ANCIENT CELTS

BARBARIANS!
ANCIENT CELTS

KATHRYN HINDS

MARSHALL CAVENDISH · BENCHMARK · NEW YORK

To Tommy, Valerie, Lisa, and Laverne

The author and publishers would like to express special thanks to Catherine McKenna,
Margaret Brooks Robinson Professor of Celtic Languages and Literatures,
Harvard University, for her gracious assistance in reviewing the manuscript of this book.

Marshall Cavendish Benchmark 99 White Plains Road Tarrytown, New York 10591
www.marshallcavendish.us
Text copyright © 2010 by Marshall Cavendish Corporation Map copyright © 2010 by Mike Reagan

LIBRARY OF CONGRESS CATALOGING-IN-PUBLICATION DATA
Hinds, Kathryn, 1962-
Ancient Celts : / by Kathryn Hinds.
p. cm. — (Barbarians!)
Includes bibliographical references and index.
Summary: "A history of the ancient Celts, from their Iron Age culture to their final conquest
by the Romans in the first century CE"—Provided by publisher. ISBN 978-0-7614-4062-8
1. Celts—Juvenile literature. I. Title. D70.H55 2009 936.4—dc22 2008035976

EDITOR: Joyce Stanton PUBLISHER: Michelle Bisson ART DIRECTOR: Anahid Hamparian
SERIES DESIGNER: Michael Nelson

Images provided by Rose Corbett Gordon, Art Editor of Mystic CT, from the following sources: Cover: The Art Archive/Musée des Beaux Arts La Rochelle/Gianni Dagli Orti Back cover: The Art Archive/Museo Civico Romano Brescia Italy Page 1: The Art Archive/Alfredo Dagli Orti; pages 2-3: Musée d'Orsay, Paris/Bridgeman Art Library; page 6: C. Walker/Topham/The Image Works; pages 8, 57: Werner Forman/Art Resource, NY; page 11: Praehistorishches Museum, Hallstatt, Austria/Bildarchiv Steffens/Bridgeman Art Library; pages 12 top, 44: The Art Archive/National Museum of Prague/Alfredo Dagli Orti; pages 12 bottom, 14 bottom, 15, 28, 37, 47, 50 & 51: Erich Lessing/Art Resource, NY; page 14 top: Musée Archeologique/Chatillan Sur Sein, France/Bridgeman Art Library; pages 16, 61, 66: Werner Forman/Corbis; pages 17, 67 top: The Art Archive/Musée des Antiquités St Germain en Laye/Gianni Dagli Orti; page 20: The Art Archive/Musée des Beaux Arts La Rochelle/Gianni Dagli Orti; page 22: The Art Archive/Museo Nazionale Atestino Este/Alfredo Dagli Orti; page 24: Musée des Beaux-Arts, Dunkirk, France/Bridgeman Art Library; page 25: akg-images; pages 27, 33, 49, 62: Private Collection/Bridgeman Art Library; page 30: Nimatallah/Art Resource, NY; page 34: Manchester Art Gallery, UK/Bridgeman Art Library; page 36: Historic Impressions, www.historicimpressions.com; page 39: Scala/Art Resource, NY; page 40: Drents Museum, the Netherlands; page 42: Max Alexander (c) Dorling Kindersley/dkimages; page 45: The Art Archive/Musée Paris/Gianni Dagli Orti; page 48: Musee Borely, Marseille, France/Lauros/Giraudon/Bridgeman Art Library; page 52: Bridgeman-Giraudon/Art Resource, NY; page 54: The Art Archive/Garrick Club/Eileen Tweedy; page 59: Mary Evans Picture Library/The Image Works; page 60: Tate, London/Art Resource, NY; page 64: age footstock/SuperStock; page 65: J. Irwin/ClassicStock/The Image Works; page 67 bottom: The Art Archive/Museo Civico Romano Brescia Italy/Alfredo Dagli Orti.

Printed in Malaysia
135642

Front cover: A conquering Celtic chief enters a Roman house, in a scene imagined by nineteenth-century French artist Paul-Joseph Jamin.
Half-title page: A Celtic god, portrayed on a silver bowl known as the Gundestrup Cauldron
Title page: Warriors guarding the coast of Gaul, painted in 1888 by French artist Jean Lecomte du Noüy.
page 6: A stone head from northern Britain, possibly used as a symbol of protection on a Celtic farm
Back cover: A silver decoration from a horse's harness, found in northern Italy and made in the second or first century BCE

CONTENTS

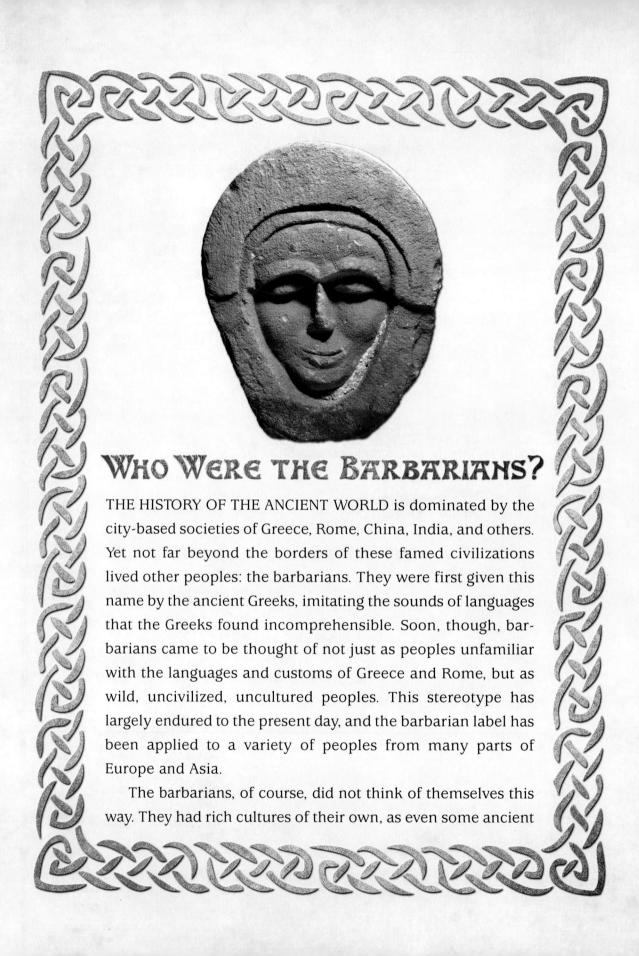

Who Were the Barbarians?

THE HISTORY OF THE ANCIENT WORLD is dominated by the city-based societies of Greece, Rome, China, India, and others. Yet not far beyond the borders of these famed civilizations lived other peoples: the barbarians. They were first given this name by the ancient Greeks, imitating the sounds of languages that the Greeks found incomprehensible. Soon, though, barbarians came to be thought of not just as peoples unfamiliar with the languages and customs of Greece and Rome, but as wild, uncivilized, uncultured peoples. This stereotype has largely endured to the present day, and the barbarian label has been applied to a variety of peoples from many parts of Europe and Asia.

The barbarians, of course, did not think of themselves this way. They had rich cultures of their own, as even some ancient writers realized. The civilized peoples both feared the barbarians and were fascinated by them. Great Greek and Roman historians such as Herodotus and Tacitus investigated and described their customs, sometimes even holding them up as examples for the people of their own sophisticated societies. Moreover, the relationships between the barbarians and civilization were varied and complex. Barbarians are most famous for raiding and invading, and these were certainly among their activities. But often the barbarians were peaceable neighbors and close allies, trading with the great cities and even serving them as soldiers and contributing to their societies in other ways.

Our information about the barbarians comes from a variety of sources: archaeology, language studies, ancient and medieval historians, and later literature. Unfortunately, though, we generally have few records in the barbarians' own words, since many of these peoples did not leave much written material. Instead we frequently learn about them from the writings of civilizations who thought of them as strange and usually inferior, and often as enemies. But modern scholars, like detectives, have been sifting through the evidence to learn more and more about these peoples and the compelling roles they played in the history of Europe, Asia, and even Africa. Now it's our turn to look beyond the borders of the familiar "great civilizations" of the past and meet the barbarians.

A variety of systems of dating have been used by different cultures throughout history. Many historians now prefer to use BCE (Before Common Era) and CE (Common Era) instead of BC (Before Christ) and AD (Anno Domini), out of respect for the diversity of the world's peoples.

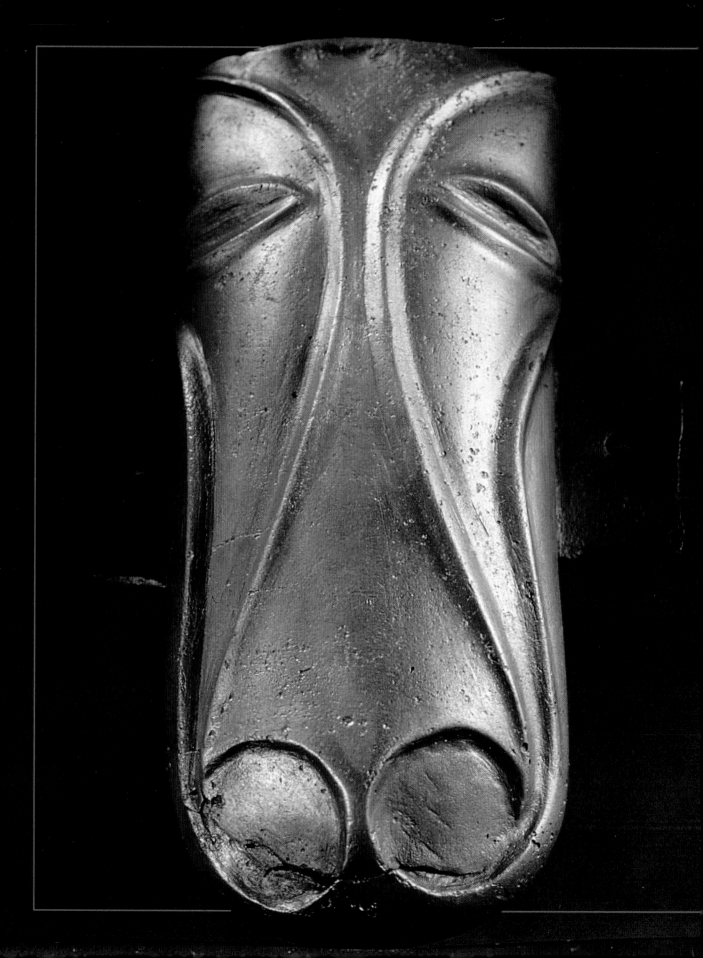

INTRODUCING the CELTS

ONE DAY IN 335 BCE A YOUNG KING NAMED ALEXANDER was camped beside the Danube River. He already ruled Greece and Macedonia, and he was setting out to conquer an empire. During a lull between battles, a group of foreign ambassadors arrived to see him. They were Celts and came from lands a little northwest of Alexander's. According to the Greek historian Strabo, "The king received them kindly and asked them, when drinking, what it was that they most feared, thinking that they would say himself, but they replied they feared nothing except that the sky might fall on them."

This was the first time Alexander had ever met any Celtic people, but he had certainly heard of them. His own teacher, the great philosopher Aristotle, had written about the bravery of the Celts, who did not even fear the powers of nature— "neither earthquakes nor waves." Aristotle thought, however, that "in general the courage of barbarians [was] compounded with high-spiritedness" and was more like madness than true courage. But on this day in 335, these Celtic ambassadors were

Opposite page: This bronze horse's face decorated the chariot of an important member of the Brigantes tribe in northern Britain during the first century CE.

9

not especially interested in demonstrating their bravery. They simply wanted a treaty of friendship with Alexander. They got it, and returned to their own land—where they kept their new friend's northern neighbors distracted with warfare so that he could get on with his conquests in the east and become Alexander the Great.

Unlike Alexander, the Celts never had a unified empire. Most of them probably didn't even think of themselves as Celts, even though they all spoke closely related languages and shared common art styles, religious traditions, and social structures. Instead they identified themselves by their tribal groups—Senones, Parisii, Aedui, Belgae, Brigantes, Silures, and many others. The numerous Celtic tribes were more likely to fight one another than to unite for any common purpose. All the same, for several hundred years they were one of the dominant peoples of Europe. They occupied territory stretching from Ireland to Asia Minor, and they threatened the might of Greece and Rome. Where did they come from, and how did they become such a force to be reckoned with?

FROM SALT MINES TO HILL FORTS

In ancient times there was a great trading network running through central Europe. Some of its most important centers were in what is now Austria, where there were stupendous deposits of salt. Salt was extremely important for preserving food, so whoever controlled the salt mines could become very wealthy and powerful. About 2,700 years ago, the salt mine owners were people who have been identified as early Celts.

There are no written records about the Celts from this time, so information about them comes from the finds of archaeologists. In the 1840s a government mining official discovered a cemetery at the Austrian town of Hallstatt. Excavating it, he found a wealth of grave goods, including swords, jewelry, and various kinds of containers. Some of the

metal objects were made of bronze, but many were iron—the cemetery dated to near the beginning of western Europe's Iron Age, around
700 BCE. In the ancient salt mines near the cemetery, archaeologists discovered more objects from the same period: wooden tools, fragments
of woolen clothing, even fur berets and a leather backpack—all remark-
ably preserved by the salt.

Austrian artists based this scene of a Hallstatt miner on archaeological finds in the salt mines.

The excavators of Hallstatt knew that by the 400s BCE Greek geographers and historians were aware that peoples they called Celts lived
in territory from Iberia (modern Spain and Portugal) to central Europe.
It was therefore not a stretch to conclude that the people of Iron Age
Hallstatt were Celts. And what was more, soon additional discoveries
were made not only in Austria but also in Germany, Switzerland, and
France. The finds closely resembled those at Hallstatt in materials, artis-
tic style, and other aspects, so scholars now spoke about a Hallstatt culture, or the Hallstatt phase of Celtic culture.

Archaeology has told us many things about this culture. The Iron Age
Celts were probably not invaders but descendants of the same people

FROM BRONZE to IRON

PREHISTORY IS GENERALLY DIVIDED INTO SEVERAL DISTINCT PHASES: the Old Stone Age (or Paleolithic), the New Stone Age (or Neolithic, when farming was introduced), the Bronze Age, and the Iron Age. Sometimes scholars also write of a Middle Stone Age and of a Copper Age occurring between the New Stone Age and the Bronze Age. All these names come from the main materials that were used to make tools. The ages were phases in the development of technology, and these phases occurred at different times in different parts of the world.

The first people to have an Iron Age were the Hittites of Asia Minor (modern Turkey). It was they who discovered how to refine iron and forge it into tools, probably a little before 1500 BCE. The new techniques gradually spread to other places, reaching Greece in the eleventh century BCE and Italy by the eighth century BCE. Ironworking may have come to the Celtic lands through Italy, or it may have come from the east, brought by horse-riding peoples who migrated from the Black Sea region along the Danube River and into what is now Hungary. Either way, the technology spread rapidly from this point and was known all the way in the west of Britain within a century.

An iron spearhead used by a first-century BCE Celtic warrior in what is now the Czech Republic

Bronze had been a fine material for tools and weapons, but iron had some major advantages. It was more durable than bronze, and it kept a sharper edge. It was also easier to work, and easier to get—it was much more abundant than the tin and copper that had to be combined to make bronze. Iron was found almost everywhere, in many forms, and often occurred near the earth's surface, so little mining was required. Some areas, of course, had larger iron deposits than others—and some of the richest iron-ore supplies in Europe were in Celtic territory.

This bronze helmet from the 400s BCE may not have been enough to protect its wearer from the heavy blows that dented it.

With plowshares tipped with iron, the Celts could farm heavier, more fertile soils. Cattle could be raised more efficiently, too, because with iron scythes hay could be easily cut to store for winter feed. And iron made excellent weapons. With iron swords and spearheads, Celtic warriors were well armed to claim lands and power and to move out from their homeland in search of greater wealth.

who had lived in the region for generation upon generation. But the coming of iron, together with new contacts and trading relationships with other peoples, changed society in many ways. New elite classes arose, including warriors of different ranks. Evidence for this class system has been found in burials. Regular warriors were buried with a long sword made for slashing, along with some personal goods. A higher rank seems to have been made up of warriors who fought on horseback, thanks to superior breeds of horses that became available from the Black Sea region. These horsemen were buried with sword, personal goods, and horse trappings of finely worked metal.

At the highest rank (as far as we can tell), warriors were buried not only with their weapons and the other usual possessions, but with heavy four-wheeled vehicles. These were probably ceremonial carts, which may have been used in the funeral procession to bear the body to its final resting place. These carts were produced with cutting-edge transportation technology developed by the Celts: Each spoked wooden wheel had a rim made from a single length of wood softened by heat so that it could be carefully bent into shape. The wheel was then strengthened and protected by a piece of iron "shrunk" into place to make a perfectly fitting iron tire.

During the 500s BCE the number of elite burials decreased across the region. This seems to indicate that a smaller number of power centers were ruling over larger territories, and power was being concentrated into the hands of fewer people. So, apparently, was wealth. More and more luxury items showed up in elite graves. One woman was buried in a dress embroidered with silk thread that came all the way from China. Most imported goods traveled a smaller distance, coming from Greek traders based in what is now southern France and Etruscan traders from northern Italy.

The most popular and prestigious items were ones associated with wine drinking: large containers for mixing wine, jugs or flagons for

The huge bronze krater buried with the "Lady of Vix," who died around 500 BCE. It weighed 460 pounds and was imported from either Greece or Etruria.

pouring it, cups for drinking it. For example, an elaborate bronze krater (a type of Greek wine jar) more than five feet tall was one of the objects buried with a woman at Vix, near the source of the Seine River. Her tomb, a wooden chamber covered over with an earthen mound, also contained other imported wine accessories, a four-wheeled cart, and a great deal of jewelry, including an amber necklace and gold torc, or neck ring. The magnificence of her burial gives the definite impression that she was someone of power and importance, quite possibly a queen who ruled the region in her own right. The size of the wine jar is an important clue to her status: leaders were expected to host splendid feasts at which there was plenty of alcohol for all their followers to drink. She was probably about thirty-five when she died.

A burial mound at Hochdorf in Germany contained a similarly rich burial, this time of a man. About forty years old and more than six feet tall, he was laid out on a bronze couch decorated with scenes of warriors riding in horse-drawn carts and fighting in single combat. He wore a torc, arm ring, belt, and dagger, all made of gold, and shoes covered in gold leaf. He also had on a conical hat fashioned from birch bark. The cart buried with him was covered in sheets of bronze and iron and piled with cups and other vessels. There were nine drinking horns in the burial chamber, and a bronze cauldron imported from Greece, large enough to hold about eighty-eight gallons. Tests have shown that the cauldron contained mead, an alcoholic drink made from honey, which was popular in Celtic lands throughout ancient and medieval times, and even beyond.

This bronze figure formed one of the legs of the couch on which the Hochdorf chief was laid to rest around 530 BCE.

The tombs of the lady of Vix and the lord of Hochdorf were close to strongholds built on top of hills that overlooked and dominated the surrounding farmland. Such hill forts were the typical headquarters of Celtic rulers. In some of these forts archaeologists have found evidence within the walls of numerous wooden houses and workshops clustered together. They may have been flimsily constructed, since in many cases they seem to have been frequently rebuilt. Fortifications often under-went renovation, too. During this period at least one hill fort received new walls built in the Greek style, probably by a Greek engineer—evidence that the ruler was not only interested in the latest ideas from abroad but could afford to pay for the services of foreign experts.

As for the common people, for the most part we can only make guesses about how they lived. There were obviously skilled artisans who crafted many of the fine objects found in the tombs. There were miners who dug up salt and metals. Most people, though, would have been farmers, raising cattle and sheep, growing barley and wheat.

A typical Hallstatt family probably lived in a thatch-roofed cabin like the building on the left. The other building is a bake-house, which could have been shared by more than one family. These reconstructions at an Austrian museum are based on the findings of archaeologists.

Women, as in most of the premodern world, would have spent a great deal of their time spinning, weaving, and sewing. Celtic women were expert weavers, even at this early time producing plaid woolen cloth similar to what much later Celts in Scotland would use to make their kilts.

ON THE THRESHOLD OF HISTORY

By the late Hallstatt era, the centers of Celtic power were mainly in what is now southern Germany. The upper class, at least, lived in relative peace, comfort, and luxury, enjoying the benefits of trade and communication with the Greeks and Etruscans. The Celts farther north, though, didn't have things quite so easy. Their neighbors were tribes of Germans and other migrating peoples with whom they often fought for land and other resources. The more northern Celts therefore seem to have had plenty of opportunity to become extremely skilled in warfare. And it is possible that eventually they used that skill in raids and other strikes against the southern Celts. In any case, archaeology shows major changes in Celtic culture starting around 450 BCE.

This first-century metal plaque from Wales pairs human faces with an abstract tree-of-life design. The combination of the human head with tendrils, leaves, and other plantlike shapes was a common feature of La Tène art.

Probably for a combination of reasons, centers of Celtic power shifted away from southern Germany and Austria. New centers developed in what are now France and Switzerland and in Bohemia (the modern Czech Republic). This new phase of Celtic culture is called La Tène, after a site in Switzerland where a great many weapons, shields, brooches, belt clasps, razors, vehicle parts, cauldrons, and other items were found in a shallow lake bed in the 1850s. These objects were decorated in a distinctive manner that remained a hallmark of Celtic art for centuries to come.

Elements of La Tène art included stylized faces and animals, fantastic creatures, leaves and other plant forms, and abstract or geometric patterns, often swirling or interlinking. One commonly used figure was the triskele, a design with three arms or branches moving in the same direction around a central point. Like many of the other elements, it almost certainly had a symbolic meaning. Some people think the three branches may have stood for earth, sea, and sky, but we will probably never know for certain.

The fine metal objects produced in the La Tène style were made largely for the warrior elite, who still headed society. These warriors and leaders not only enjoyed new fashions in art but were being buried with some new kinds of grave goods (in addition to the traditional wine-drinking equipment). Instead of four-wheeled carts, they had light, maneuverable two-wheeled chariots. Most chariot burials were of men, but there were some of women, suggesting that they could occasionally play a role in military leadership. And whereas late Hallstatt-period warriors were buried with weapons that seemed to be mainly for hunting or ceremonial display, La Tène warriors took to their graves an array of weapons of war: shields, helmets, swords, spears, bows, and arrows.

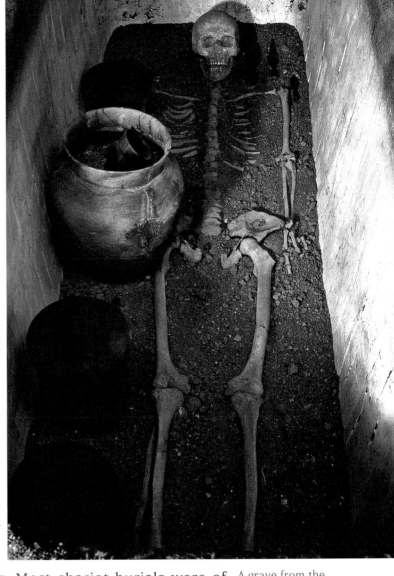

A grave from the La Tène period. A spearhead lies beside the skeleton's head, as if the deceased was buried holding a spear over his shoulder, the same way he would have carried it in life.

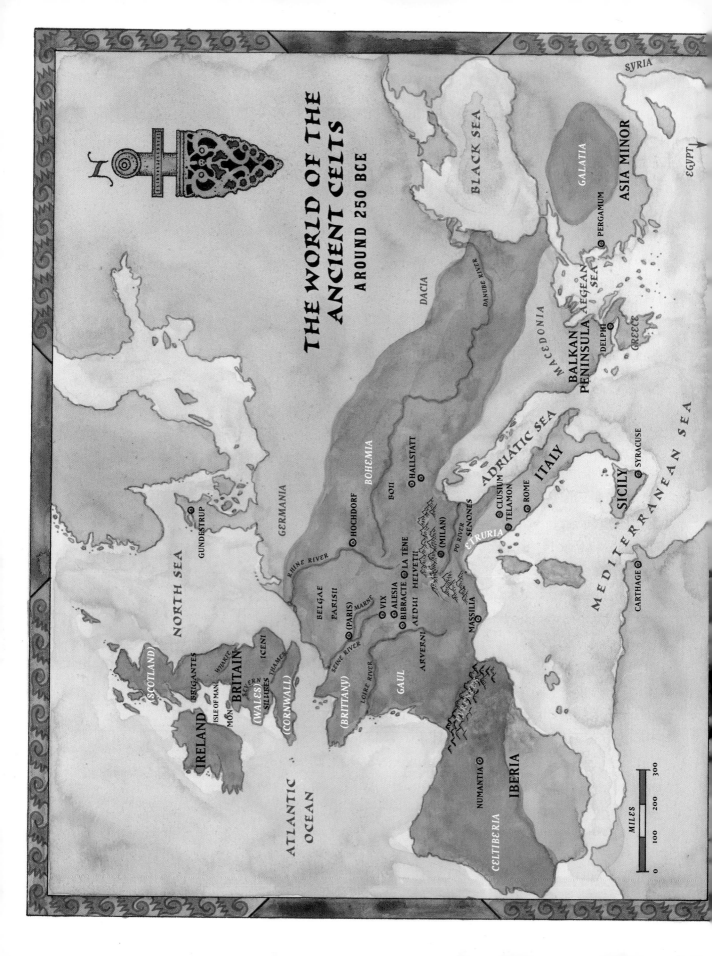

THE WORLD OF THE ANCIENT CELTS

AROUND 250 BCE

SYRIA

BLACK SEA

GALATIA

ASIA MINOR

EGYPT

PERGAMUM

AEGEAN SEA

DELPHI

GREECE

MACEDONIA

BALKAN PENINSULA

DACIA

DANUBE RIVER

ADRIATIC SEA

ITALY

SICILY

SYRACUSE

MEDITERRANEAN SEA

CARTHAGE

ROME

TELAMON

CLUSIUM

ETRURIA

MASSILIA

PO RIVER

SENONES

(MILAN)

HELVETII

LA TÈNE

AEDUI

BIBRACTE

ALESIA

VIX

HALLSTATT

BOII

BOHEMIA

HOCHDORF

RHINE RIVER

GERMANIA

GUNDESTRUP

NORTH SEA

BELGAE

PARISII

(PARIS)

MARNE

SEINE RIVER

LOIRE RIVER

ARVERNI

GAUL

(BRITTANY)

(CORNWALL)

SILURES

THAMES

(WALES)

SEVERN

MÔN

ISLE OF MAN

BRITAIN

(SCOTLAND)

BRIGANTES

WHARFE

ICENI

IRELAND

ATLANTIC OCEAN

IBERIA

CELTIBERIA

NUMANTIA

MILES

0   100   200   300

Times were unsettled; things were changing. As just one example, around 400 BCE the salt mine at Hallstatt ceased operating. In addition, population in the Celtic lands was increasing rapidly, straining resources. Raids on neighboring tribes and peoples, especially in outlying areas, were probably on the rise. There was an ever greater need for fresh grazing and farmland. Warriors began to fight their way into new territory, followed by their families, herds, and cartloads of possessions.

Sometimes it was only small bands on the move; sometimes large tribal groups migrated into new areas. They went west, east, and north. But the most tempting direction was south, into the rich lands of Italy. More than three centuries later, Roman author Pliny the Elder explained the temptation; like most Romans, he referred to the Celts as Gauls, a word that may originally have meant "foreigners" or "enemies":

> The Gauls, imprisoned as they were by the Alps . . . first found a motive for overflowing into Italy from the circumstance of a Gallic citizen from Switzerland named Helico who had lived in Rome because of his skill as a craftsman, [and] brought with him, when he came back, some dried figs and grapes and some samples of oil and wine: consequently we may excuse them [the Celts] for having sought to obtain these things even by means of war.

Pliny's story was probably just a folktale. But the fact was that Celts did migrate into Italy on a large scale around 400 BCE. This migration would soon bring them into contact with their greatest enemies: the Romans.

INTO ITALY

T HE HISTORIAN TITUS LIVIUS, OR LIVY (57 BCE–17 CE), WAS ONE of many Roman authors who wrote about the Celts. He drew on a variety of old stories, not all of which were strictly accurate. But most held at least a kernel of truth, and perhaps more. For example, there was one about a Celtic king named Ambigatus, who ruled a portion of Gaul (as the Romans called modern France, Belgium, and parts of Germany and Switzerland):

Gaul under his sway grew so rich in corn [grain] and so populous, that it seemed hardly possible to govern so great a multitude. The king, now old, wishing to relieve his kingdom of a burdensome throng, announced that he meant to send Bellovesus and Segovesus, his sister's two sons, two enterprising young men, to find such homes as the gods might assign to them . . . and promised them that they should head as large a number of emigrants as they themselves desired, so that no tribe

Opposite page: An imaginative portrayal of Brennus, the chief who led the Celtic sack of Rome in 390 BCE

21

might be able to prevent their settlement. Whereupon to Segovesus were by lot assigned the Hercynian highlands [Bohemia and the Black Forest region of Germany], but to Bellovesus the gods proposed a far pleasanter road, into Italy. Taking with him the surplus population . . . he set out with a vast host, some mounted, some on foot.

Livy claimed that these events occurred around 600 BCE—and indeed, archaeologists in northern Italy have found Celtic-language inscriptions that seem to date back to about that period. There may well have been a small Celtic community living between Etruscan lands and the Alps for some time—these Celts could have been of great help in enabling trade between the Etruscans and the Celts on the other side of the mountains. In any case, the Celtic presence in north Italy was about to get a lot bigger.

OVER THE MOUNTAINS

Around 400 BCE Celts from about half a dozen tribes began to pour over the Alps into the area around the Po River. This rich, fertile valley was already occupied by Etruscans and other Italian peoples. Most were quickly overcome by the Celtic warriors, and the victorious Celts settled down. Each tribal group claimed its own territory and founded villages and small towns—some of which later developed into great Italian cities such as

A Celtic woman from northern Italy. She seems to wear her hair in a thick braid down her back, and her elaborately patterned dress may be a special ceremonial garment.

Milan and Verona. The Greek historian Polybius (ca. 200–ca. 118 BCE) wrote that these Celts

> lived in open villages, and without any permanent buildings. As they made their beds of straw or leaves, and fed on meat, and followed no pursuits but those of war and agriculture, they lived simple lives without being acquainted with any science or art whatever. Each man's property, moreover, consisted in cattle and gold; as they were the only things that could be easily carried with them, when they wandered from place to place, and changed their dwelling as their fancy directed. They made a great point, however, of friendship; for the man who had the largest number of clients or companions in his wandering was looked upon as the most formidable and powerful member of the tribe.

Polybius seems to be describing an early phase of settlement, or he may have based his description largely on warriors' encampments or perhaps on the temporary shelters that shepherds used as they drove sheep to different pastures in different seasons. As a whole, in any case, the Celts certainly were not without science and art. On the other hand, Polybius's comments about friendship and the bonds of loyalty among leaders and their followers are echoed in many other sources about the ancient Celts. This kind of loyalty was a feature of later Celtic culture, too.

TUMULT

Celts continued to migrate across the Alps, often warring with the Celts who were already in northern Italy. Before long, many of the Celts in the Po valley began to move south and west again in search of more land. In about 390* BCE, according to Livy, the citizens of the Etruscan

*This is the traditional date, but many historians now think these events probably occurred in 387 or 386 BCE.

Celtic warriors advance through the Italian countryside, alarming the citizens of Clusium and Rome.

city of Clusium were threatened by "strange men in thousands . . . men the like of whom the townsfolk had never seen, outlandish warriors armed with strange weapons."

The Etruscans sent to Rome for help negotiating with the Celts, who demanded land to settle on, or they would attack. Livy reports that when the Romans asked what right the Celts had to make such an ultimatum, "the haughty answer was returned that they carried their right in their weapons, and that everything belonged to the brave." Tempers rose after this, with fighting quickly breaking out—and the Roman ambassadors, who were supposed to remain peacefully impartial, joined in the battle. The Celts viewed this as dishonorable and were insulted. Plus, they weren't successful in getting land or loot from Clusium. They decided instead to attack Rome, some eighty miles to the south.

Led by a warrior with the name or title Brennus, the Celts advanced. Eleven miles from the great city, they crushed the Roman army's desperate attempt to stop them. Fear struck Rome; many people fled, and the remaining able-bodied citizens took refuge on the fortified hill of the Capitol. The Celts marched into the wide-open city and thoroughly plundered it. They then besieged the Capitol until the Romans paid them a tribute of one thousand pounds of gold—a tremendous sum, but it got the Celts to go back to northern Italy.

For hundreds of years afterward, the Romans vividly recalled the horror of their first encounters with the Celts. They called it the *tumultus*, the "panic" or "national emergency." It became part of Roman folklore, and Roman paranoia. Every child knew the stories: how the old men remained seated in front of their houses, still as statues until a Celt pulled one's beard to see if he was real; how the Celts respectfully left a brave priest unharmed when he came down from the Capitol to perform a religious ceremony; how the geese sacred to the goddess Juno honked an alarm to save the besieged Romans from a band of Celts sneaking up to the Capitol at night. And then there was the weighing out of the thousand pounds of gold. The Romans believed that the Celts were using inaccurate weights, and complained. Brennus responded by throwing his sword onto the scale, "with an exclamation intolerable to Roman ears, 'Woe to the vanquished!'" It was no wonder that the Celts went down in Roman history as the barbarians to whom all other barbarians would be compared.

A French engraving of Brennus adding his sword to the scales weighing out the Roman tribute, just before his famous exclamation of "Woe to the vanquished!"

THE LONG AFTERMATH

For decades the Celts continued to live up to their terrible reputation, making repeated raids in Italy. During this time the Celts also demonstrated their usefulness as mercenaries—hired warriors. The powerful rulers of the Greek city-state of Syracuse, on the island of Sicily, did not like the way Rome was enlarging its territory. On many occasions they encouraged and even employed Celtic forces to harass Rome and its allies. The Celts were regarded as such a menace that in 285 BCE Rome brutally exterminated an entire Celtic tribe, the Senones. No doubt the Romans were also motivated by the desire to take over the Senones' territory, a stretch of very fertile farmland along the Adriatic coast.

Two years later the Boii tribe joined with an Etruscan army to challenge Rome, but they were horribly defeated. An uneasy peace followed, and Rome proceeded to bring more and more of the Italian Peninsula under its rule. Meanwhile there was unrest among the remaining tribes of northern Italy. They had to deal with shifting alliances among themselves, more bands of Celts crossing the Alps, and even the assassination of two tribal kings. Moreover, the new generation of warriors coming into power were urging fresh attacks against Rome, both because they wanted land and plunder and because they felt threatened by Rome's growth.

In 225 BCE warriors drawn from at least three tribes marched on Rome again. The Celtic army also included a large group of fighters from across the Alps called Gaesatae, positioned in the front lines. While the other Celts went into battle wearing light cloaks and leather breeches, the Gaesatae fought naked, protected by nothing but their shields. Polybius described the combined Celtic forces this way:

There were among them such innumerable horns and trumpets, which were being blown simultaneously in all parts of their

A LASTING STEREOTYPE

These Celtic warriors are dressed in the style described by ancient writers. The leader's helmet and shield are based on first-century BCE arms found near London.

THE MEDITERRANEAN WORLD'S EARLY experiences with the Celts made a deep impression, leaving people with stereotyped images that would not go away. For centuries Greek and Roman geographers and historians wrote the same kinds of things, over and over, about the Celts. Here, for example, is a selection from the Greek geographer Strabo (ca. 64 BCE– ca. 23 CE):

The whole race . . . is madly fond of war, high-spirited and quick to battle. . . . And so when they are stirred up they assemble in their bands for battle, quite openly and without forethought, so that they are easily handled by those who desire to outwit them; for at any time or place and on whatever pretext you stir them up, you will have them ready to face danger, even if they have nothing on their side but their own strength and courage.

Diodorus Siculus, writing in the first century BCE, commented on another stereotyped Celtic trait: "The Gauls are exceedingly addicted to the use of wine and fill themselves with the wine which is brought into their country by merchants . . . and since they partake of this drink without moderation by reason of their craving for it, when they are drunken they fall into a stupor or a state of madness." Later in his *Library of History*, Diodorus added some remarks about the Celts' appearance and table manners: "They look like wood-demons, their hair thick and shaggy like a horse's mane. Some of them are clean-shaven, but others—especially those of high rank—shave their cheeks but leave a moustache that covers the whole mouth and, when they eat and drink, acts like a sieve, trapping particles of food."

Celts often went into battle accompanied by musicians playing animal-headed trumpets like these. The warrior in front of the trumpeters has a crest on his helmet in the shape of a boar, an animal honored for its toughness and fierceness.

army, and their cries were so loud and piercing, that the noise seemed not to come merely from trumpets and human voices, but from the whole countryside at once. Not less terrifying was the appearance and rapid movement of the naked warriors in the van [advance guard], which indicated men in the prime of their strength . . . while all the warriors in the front ranks were richly adorned with gold necklaces [torcs] and bracelets. These sights certainly dismayed the Romans.

When the Celtic and Roman armies met at Telamon, north of Rome, the Celts prevailed at first. But the Roman troops were more numerous and far more disciplined. In the end, 40,000 Celts were killed and another 10,000 were taken back to Rome as slaves.

It was a crushing defeat, and opened the way for the Romans to carry out their plan to rid Italy of the Celts for good. They systematically attacked and destroyed Celtic settlements, killing or driving off the inhabitants. The Second Punic War (218–201 BCE), between Rome and Carthage, at first interrupted this project, then gave the Romans even more reason for it: large numbers of Celtic warriors fought for the Carthaginian general Hannibal when he invaded Italy. But Hannibal was finally defeated, and the Romans turned back to ending the Celtic threat.

The Romans now felt secure in their ability to overcome the Celts. As Polybius wrote,

> They had learned from former engagements that Gallic tribes were always most formidable at the first onslaught, before their courage was at all damped . . . and that the swords with which they were furnished . . . could only give one downward cut with any effect, but that after this the edges got so turned and the blade so bent, that unless they had time to straighten them with their foot against the ground, they could not deliver a second blow. . . . The Romans closed with them, and rendered them quite helpless, by preventing them from raising their hands to strike with their swords, which is their peculiar and only stroke, because their blade has no point. The Romans, on the contrary, having excellent points to their swords, used them not to cut but to thrust: and by thus repeatedly hitting the breasts and faces of the enemy, they eventually killed the greater number of them.

By 190 BCE northern Italy belonged to Roman colonists. The remaining Celtic farmers became assimilated into Roman society, adopting more and more aspects of Roman culture.

At least one Celtic tradition, however, seems to have lived on: the love of poetry, and skill in composing it. A number of Rome's greatest poets (and other writers as well) came from the once-Celtic region of Italy. Coincidence? Perhaps; perhaps not. In any case, it is nice to think that some remaining Celtic spirit lingered on there, inspiring the creation of some of the world's most enduring literature.

The Celtic leader Catumandus recognized the power of the Roman goddess Minerva (the Greeks called her Athena). According to later writers, many Celts worshipped a goddess very similar to Minerva.

3

AMONG the GREEKS

NOT LONG BEFORE THE SACK OF ROME, ANOTHER MEDITERRANEAN city was under Celtic threat. This was Massilia (now Marseille, France), a prosperous Greek trading colony—and source of many of the luxury imports that aristocratic Celts had long enjoyed. But earlier friendly relations with the Greeks of Massilia were temporarily forgotten, according to a story told by Pompeius Trogus in the late first century BCE. The son of a Celt who was a Roman citizen, Trogus gave history a valuable portrayal of Celtic ways of thinking:

> Massilia was flourishing in abundance of wealth, distinction of achievements and the increasing glory of her strength, [so] the neighbouring peoples gathered for the purpose of eliminating her very name. . . . The tribal [Celtic] king Catumandus was elected leader by general agreement. When he was laying siege to the city with a great army of his choicest warriors, he was terrified in his sleep by the vision of a menacing woman who said

she was a goddess, and he straight away made peace with the Massiliotes. He asked if he might be allowed to enter the city to pay his worship to the gods of the city. When he came to the temple of Minerva [goddess of war and crafts] on the citadel, he saw . . . a statue of the goddess he had seen in his dream. . . . He congratulated the Massiliotes for being under the protection of the immortal gods, and he presented the goddess with a golden torque and made a treaty of perpetual friendship with the Massiliotes.

The Celtic leader's belief in signs from the gods and his respect for the divine will saved the day for Massilia. Other parts of the Greek world, however, did not get off so lightly.

THE CITY OF APOLLO

By 300 BCE many waves of Celtic immigrants had followed the Danube River eastward from the Celtic heartland and settled in the northern part of the Balkan Peninsula. In 298 a Celtic chief led his warriors south into Macedonia, but was driven back. In the following years, however, the Celtic desire to win gold and glory in the Greek lands increased. Ambitious young warriors were no doubt fired up by stories about the wealthy cities and richly adorned temples. In 281 three Celtic armies began the invasion of Macedonia and Greece. It faltered for unknown reasons, but one of its leaders determined to try again. Like the chief who led the sack of Rome, he was called Brennus.

Brennus's goal was Delphi, where all the great cities of Greece had their treasuries. In addition, the temples of Delphi contained centuries' worth of offerings from victorious generals, winning Olympic athletes, and ordinary citizens expressing their gratitude to the gods. The idea of all these riches drove Brennus and his warriors to endure great

An artist's reconstruction of Apollo's temple at Delphi in its prime, with Mount Parnassus towering above

hardships on their way south—and to be merciless to the people of the towns and villages they passed through. The Greeks fought desperately to stop the Celtic advance. Although they didn't succeed, they did manage to kill a large number of the enemy. Still, Brennus may have had as many as 30,000 warriors as he finally neared his goal.

Delphi was not just one of the wealthiest places of the Greek world, it was also one of the holiest. It was home to the temple of Apollo that housed the Delphic Oracle. This oracle was a priestess called the Pythia, who channeled the god's wisdom while she was in a trance. People came from all over to ask her questions—but often the guidance contained in her inspired words was none too clear. On this occasion, however, it was. With the Celts approaching, the terrified Delphians asked the oracle what they should do, and the Pythia gave them Apollo's answer: "I will defend my own."

The Greeks must have felt that Apollo kept his word, because as the Celts attacked Delphi, they were met by one natural disaster after another. The historian Pausanias told what happened this way:

The Pythia, painted in 1868 by English artist Edward Burne-Jones, beside a tripod on which laurel leaves burn in offering to Apollo

Portents boding no good to the barbarians were sent by the god, the clearest recorded in history. For the whole ground occupied by the Gallic army was shaken violently most of the day, with continuous thunder and lightning.

The thunder both terrified the Gauls and prevented them hearing their orders, while the bolts from heaven set on fire not only those whom they struck but also their neighbors, themselves and their armour alike. . . .

All the day the barbarians were beset by calamities and terrors of this kind. But the night was to bring upon them experiences far more painful. For there came on a severe frost, and snow with it, and great rocks slipping from [Mount] Parnassus, and crags breaking away, made the barbarians their target, the crash of which brought destruction, not on one or two at a time, but on thirty or even more, as they chanced to be gathered in groups keeping guard or taking rest.

After this terrible night, the Greeks surprised the Celts, attacking their rear-guard, and a furious battle ensued. During the fighting Brennus was wounded and carried off the field. With that his followers lost their fighting spirit, and soon the Celts were retreating, pursued north by the vengeful Greeks. Many more Celtic warriors were killed, and Brennus, seeing his men dying and his expedition a dishonorable failure, killed himself.

But was the expedition a complete failure? The Greek historians gave conflicting reports—while some wrote that the Celts did not reach Delphi's temples and succeed in plundering them, others maintained that they did. There are a few modern historians, too, who doubt that the Celts actually raided the holy city. Nevertheless, the Greek poet Callimachus, who lived during this time, described the Celts standing among the tripods of Apollo's temple. Strabo said the treasure of Delphi eventually ended up in Gaul, much of it sunk in a lake as an offering to the gods. And Diodorus Siculus told how Brennus entered a temple in Delphi and "laughed at them (the Greeks), to think that men, believing that gods have human form, should set up their images in wood and stone."

INTO ASIA AND AFRICA

After Brennus's death, most of his surviving warriors escaped from Greece and settled with their families in the Danube region. A number of these Danubian Celts seem to have eventually moved back west into Gaul. Members of three tribes, however, journeyed farther east. In 278 BCE these groups—about 20,000 men, women, and children in all—entered Asia Minor, where several Greek kingdoms were vying for supremacy. The ruler of one of these kingdoms welcomed the Celts as his allies, inviting the warriors to raid his neighbors to their hearts' content. They did so with enthusiasm for the next several years, until the king of one of the territories they'd been raiding put a stop to their activities. His army defeated the Celts in battle partly with the help of elephants, animals that amazed and terrified the Celts, who had never seen them before.

JULIUS CAESAR WROTE, "THE WHOLE GALLIC PEOPLE IS EXCEEDINGLY GIVEN TO RELIGIOUS superstition." It was an opinion shared by many in the Greco-Roman world, although Greeks and Romans also accused each other of being superstitious. So we can probably assume that *superstition* was used to mean enthusiastically followed religious practices, the reasons for which were not understood by the people describing them. And ancient Celtic religion had many features that not only baffled the Greeks and Romans but are difficult for scholars to explain today.

CELTIC RELIGION

Brennus's reaction to the statues of the Greek gods in Delphi tells us that at least some groups of Celts did not think of their deities as having human form. Other evidence shows that many features of the natural world were thought to be divine in some sense: for example, the sun, the moon, thunder, and bodies of water. The Celtic names of numerous rivers were also the names of goddesses, such as Sequana (the Seine) and Matrona (the Marne) in Gaul, and Sabrina (the Severn) and Verbeia (the Wharfe) in Britain. Much Celtic artwork, together with later literature, suggests that deities often took the forms of various animals, especially stags, bulls, horses, wild boars, ravens, and geese or swans.

By the mid-first century BCE, the Celts of Gaul were worshipping several important deities and portraying them in human form. These included a god of healing, a god of war, a god of the heavens, and a goddess of arts, crafts, and warfare. The most popu-

Above: Many Celts worshipped a horned or antlered god of animals and abundance.

lar god was, in Caesar's words, one whom the Celts regarded "as the inventor of all the arts, as their guide on the roads and in travel, and as chiefly influential in making money and in trade." Caesar called this god by the Roman name Mercury, but his Gaulish name was almost certainly Lugos. Under slightly different names, he was worshipped all across the Celtic world. Mother goddesses were also of great importance and went by a number of names; often they were simply called the Mothers, and they were frequently portrayed as groups of two or three women.

We know very little about how the Celts worshipped their deities. We do know they frequently made offerings by throwing objects—including valuable jewelry and weapons—into lakes, springs, and rivers. Like most ancient peoples, they also made sacrifices of animals, which would then have provided the meat

Warriors undergo a ritual of self-sacrifice.

eaten at religious feasts. From time to time the Celts sacrificed humans, too (a practice the Romans criticized as especially barbaric, even though they occasionally practiced it themselves—and they routinely presented bloody executions as popular entertainment). Human sacrifice was probably carried out mainly in times of urgent need, and the victims were generally criminals or prisoners of war.

Although many Celts knew how to read and write, and used Greek and Roman letters for everyday purposes, they did not believe in writing down anything to do with their religion. But Caesar and others picked up and passed on some bits of Celtic belief. The Celts of Gaul and Britain had religious leaders called druids, and one of their most important teachings was the immortality of the soul. As the Roman poet Lucan said, imagining that he was speaking to a group of druids, "It is you who say that the shades of the dead seek not the silent land . . . and the pale halls of [the god of the dead]; rather, you tell us that the same spirit has a body again elsewhere, and that death, if what you sing is true, is but the mid-point of long life."

The Celts were determined to stay, however. Encouraged by the ruler of yet another kingdom, they moved to a mountainous area in central Asia Minor. This region became known as Galatia (from *Galatae*, a Greek name for the Celts). Here, the historian Justinus wrote, "the numbers of Galatians grew so great that they filled Asia Minor like a swarm. In the end, none of the eastern kings would fight a war without hiring Galatian mercenaries." Galatians fought for the kings of Greece, Macedonia, Syria, and most of the kings of Asia Minor. But the "eastern kings" who relied most on the Galatians were probably those who ruled Egypt.

The first Celts in Egypt were four thousand mercenaries hired by King Ptolemy II, probably in the 270s BCE, to help fight his rebellious half brother. According to Pausanias, soon after arrival the Celts plotted "to seize Egypt," and so Ptolemy marooned them on a deserted island in the Nile River. "There they perished at one another's hands or by famine." Nevertheless, Galatian mercenaries went on serving the rulers of Egypt generation after generation, right up until the death of Cleopatra in 30 BCE.

Along with working as hired warriors, the Galatians continued to conduct raids on their own behalf. They carried off not only plunder but people, whom they held for ransom or sold as slaves. In addition they blackmailed wealthy cities, demanding gold in exchange for leaving them in peace. Finally King Attalus I of Pergamum had had enough and decided to put an end to the Celts' marauding and blackmailing—and he had an army strong enough to do so. Around 233 BCE he defeated the Celts in a battle that made him a hero throughout the Greek world. He commemorated his victory with a group of bronze statues showing the Celts in defeat. These statues no longer exist, but marble copies sculpted by the Romans do, and they remain some of the most renowned and moving images of the ancient Celts ever made.

Even after their defeat by Attalus, the three Galatian tribes flourished. Strabo recorded some details of their government, which seems to have had a well-developed system of checks and balances:

This life-size marble statue, known as *The Dying Gaul*, is a Roman copy of one of the bronze statues Attalus I had made to celebrate his victory over the Galatians. The warrior wears a torc around his neck, and his hair has been stiffened with lime, just as ancient writers described.

> Each tribe was divided into four sections, called tetrarchies— each of these having one tetrarch, one judge, one general (under the tetrarchs' authority), and two lesser military commanders. The twelve tetrarchs together presided over an assembly of three hundred men. These all gathered at a place called the Drunemeton. The assembly judged murder cases, but the tetrarchs and judges ruled on all other disputes.

In 190 BCE the Galatians allied with one of the "eastern kings" in a battle against Rome. The Romans won, and then attacked Galatia, where they were also victorious. They left, however, after taking 40,000 prisoners and requiring the Galatians to stop raiding western and northern Asia Minor. The Galatians complied and remained independent and

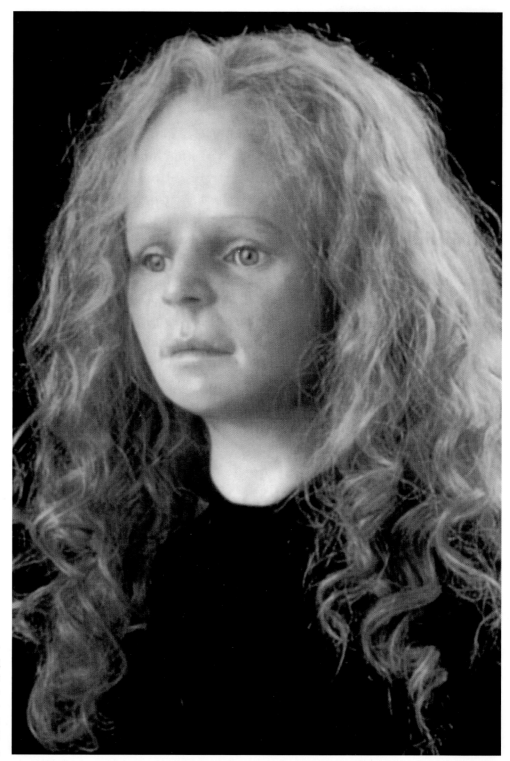

A Celtic girl, discovered in a peat bog in what is today the Netherlands. Scientists have reconstructed her face in a sensitive and realistic way.

strong for another century. But in 88 BCE, a neighboring king invited the tetrarchs and other Galatian nobles to a feast and slaughtered nearly all of them. Since that king was an enemy of Rome, the Galatians became Roman allies and then, in 67 BCE, Roman subjects.

NEW RUN-INS WITH ROME

The Galatians were not the first group of Celts to lose their independence to Rome. After the Second Punic War, Rome took over Carthage's lands in the Iberian Peninsula. North of those lands lived the Celtiberians, a Celtic-speaking people who were a fusion of the original inhabitants and Celtic immigrants who had arrived around 500 BCE. The Celtiberians and the Romans fought a number of battles and wars over several decades. In 133 BCE 60,000 Roman soldiers besieged the Celtiberians' main city, Numantia, and starved its defenders into submission. The entire surviving population was sold into slavery, the city was destroyed, and Rome went on to conquer the rest of Celtiberia.

The Romans still had a problem, however. To get to their Iberian possessions by land, they had to pass through Celtic territory in southern Gaul. An opportunity soon arose to change this situation. In 125 BCE a Celtic tribe attacked Massilia, which called on its ally, Rome, for help. A Roman army came to defend the city and soundly defeated the Celts. With a foothold in the area, the Romans forcefully pressed their advantage. By 120 BCE a large portion of southern Gaul had become a Roman province.

The next decades were extremely unsettled ones for the Celts of the European continent. They were pressured by ever more aggressive Germanic tribes in the north and by the rising Dacian culture in the east (in what is now Romania). Many tribes were on the move. But things had changed a lot since the last period of widespread Celtic migration. Rome was now the major power in the Mediterranean, and it wasn't about to allow the Celts to cause another tumult in its territories.

LIFE and LOSS in GAUL

SOMETIME IN THE NINETIES BCE, A GREEK PHILOSOPHER named Posidonius made a lengthy visit to Gaul. He met and talked with many Celts, observing them in both war and peace. Unfortunately, most of the book he wrote about his Celtic experiences has been lost. Fortunately, the book was read by later authors—Strabo, Diodorus Siculus, and Julius Caesar among them—and they passed on many of Posidonius's observations. It was from Posidonius, for example, that Diodorus Siculus learned that "the clothing of the Gauls is stunning. They wear long shirts dyed in various colors and pants that they call *bracae* [breeches]. Around their necks they fasten cloaks flowing in stripes or decorated with checkerboard squares." Posidonius also described Celtic shields, helmets, war trumpets, weapons, and chain mail (apparently a Celtic invention) with great accuracy, as archaeological finds have proven.

"LONG-HAIRED GAUL"

That is the translation of *Gallia Comata*, a Roman nickname for the territory north of the Roman province in southern Gaul. This independ-

Opposite page: A nineteenth-century statue of the Gaulish chief Vercingetorix stands on the site where he fought his final battle against the Romans.

43

ent Gaul and its people—including its long-haired warriors—were what Posidonius traveled to see and report on. He found that "the people dwell in great houses arched, constructed of planks and wicker, and covered with a heavy thatched roof. They have sheep and swine in abundance." The main foods were "milk and all kinds of flesh, especially that of swine, which they eat both fresh and salted. Their swine live in the fields, and surpass in height, strength and swiftness." Indeed, ancient Celtic art shows the important place pigs (especially wild boar) had in Celtic life and culture, and in medieval Celtic literature pork is almost always the favorite food of heroes.

Wild boar, symbols of strength and power, were often portrayed in Celtic art.

Celtic farmers also raised crops, including grain. They used hand tools—sickles, scythes, spades, pitchforks, axes—with iron blades fixed to wooden handles by a technique perfected by Celtic craftsmen. (The designs of such tools have remained pretty much the same ever since.) Their iron-tipped plows, pulled by cattle, were angled to cut through almost any type of soil. In addition, farmers of Posidonius's time may already have been using the harvesting machine—a Celtic invention—that was described in the first century CE by Pliny the Elder: "In the provinces of Gaul very large frames fitted with teeth at the edge, and carried on two wheels, are driven through the corn [grain] by a team of oxen pushing from behind."* After harvest, the grain was often stored in pits in the ground, ingeniously constructed to keep out moisture, bacteria, mold, and anything else that might cause spoilage.

Although most people in Gaul (as elsewhere before the modern era) lived in rural areas and worked the land, there were cities. The largest

*This harvesting machine was unknown anywhere else in the Roman Empire, and even in Gaul farmers seem to have stopped using it not long after the third century CE. It took till 1831 for the mechanical harvester to be reinvented.

CELTIC LEADERS SHOWED THEIR WEALTH, INFLUENCE, AND GENEROSITY BY GIVING splendid feasts. Sometimes these were for the benefit of the entire community. For example, a Greek writer of the third century BCE told how a Galatian nobleman named Ariamnes decided to treat the whole country to a year-long feast: "He divided the land into sections, all marked out at suitable distances along the roads. At every station, he built

FEASTING

a feasting hall . . . that held four hundred men or more. . . . Ariamnes then provided oxen, pigs, sheep, and every other kind of meat daily for the feasts, along with count- less jars of wine and loaves of bread." Ariamnes welcomed not just his own people but also travelers and passersby to his feasts. This kind of hospitality was a long-standing

feature of Celtic society. Diodorus Siculus noted that the Celts "invite strangers to their banquets, and only after the meal do they ask who they are and of what they stand in need."

Many feasts were mainly for warriors and other leading men of the community. Posidonius seems to have attended some feasts of this nature during his travels in Gaul. From him we learn, "When a large number dine together, they sit around in a circle with the most influential man at the center. . . . Beside him sits the host and next, on either side, the others in order of distinc- tion. Their shieldsmen stand behind them while their spearmen are seated in a circle on the opposite side and feast in common like their lords." It was the practice at such feasts for the host to give the choicest cut of meat to the bravest warrior—or for that

A feast in the Parisii tribe's capital, now known as Paris

piece of meat to be claimed by the man who considered himself the best. Either way, if everyone agreed about who deserved the "hero's portion," there was no problem. But if another man challenged him, the two would engage in single combat. A lot of wine was usually served on these occasions, sometimes leading to a dangerous mix of drunkenness and hot tempers. It was not unknown for single combats and mock bat- tles at feasts to lead to serious injury or even death.

seem to have been in what is now southern Germany—one of them had a rampart five miles around that required sixty tons of iron to make the nails that held the timbers in place. In central France, archaeologists have been excavating Bibracte, the major city of the Aedui tribe. Their discoveries show that numerous artisans and tradespeople lived and worked there. Among other things, they crafted and sold iron tools and goods (the iron was mined nearby), jewelry of several kinds, glass, and a variety of items decorated with colored enamel. In addition, they minted gold and silver coins. Judging from the number of clay wine jars, a great deal of wine trading may also have gone on in Bibracte. On the other hand, perhaps extralarge amounts of wine were consumed there because it was a center of ceremony and government—we know, for example, that Bibracte was a site where tribal councils met.

Each Gaulish tribe was self-governing, and there were two basic forms of government. In the older, traditional form the tribe was ruled by a *rix*—a king or chief. The *rix* did not automatically inherit his rank from his father. It appears he was chosen by the high-ranking warriors of the tribe, and they could select whichever member of the royal family they thought would be the best leader. In the southern half of Gaul, however, the tribes were embracing a newer type of government, probably influenced by their contact with the Greeks and Romans. In this form, a tribal council elected one or more magistrates every year, and these officials had absolute authority during their term of office. If, however, two or more tribes joined together to fight a war, they might choose one man to temporarily act as *rix* to lead the combined armies.

When Posidonius visited Gaul, warfare between the different tribes was common. Generally, though, it appears to have been a kind of limited warfare. There was no destruction of towns or crops, no killing or harming of noncombatants. The battles were contests between small groups of noble warriors who fought according to a shared code of honor, which they had been trained in since childhood. Although the winners took the arms, horses, and jewelry of the losers, the ultimate prize was the glory of victory, and the hope that generations of bards would pass on songs and tales of the victors' heroic deeds.

To win even greater glory—and to prevent the loss of too many fighting men—warriors often engaged in single combat, as Diodorus learned from Posidonius:

> When Gaulish warriors face each other in battle, one will often come forward from his lines and challenge the best man of his opponents to fight him alone. This challenger will show off his weapons and try to strike fear in the hearts of his enemies. If someone accepts the challenge, this warrior in turn will begin boasting of his brave ancestors while he belittles his opponent—all in a mutual attempt to intimidate the other side.

A bronze buckle from the sixth century BCE shows two warriors training for hand-to-hand combat.

In earlier times the Romans had seen this for themselves, and some Roman commanders had even accepted Celtic challenges to single combat. But it was not the Roman style of warfare, especially not after the Roman army was completely reorganized at the end of the second century BCE. Transformed from a body of citizens who were called up for temporary military duty as needed, it was now a full-time professional fighting force. Training and discipline were even stronger than before, and so was the might of Rome—as the Celts were about to discover.

"THE GAULS PRACTICE A CUSTOM COMMON TO MANY NORTHERN TRIBES," STRABO reported. "In battle, they hang the heads of their slain enemies around the necks of their horses, then at home they hang them on pegs in their houses. Posidonius says he frequently saw the Gauls do this and was sickened at first but got used to it eventually."

Diodorus Siculus added further information, no doubt also learned from Posidonius: "They embalm in cedar oil the heads of the most distinguished enemies, and preserve them carefully in a chest and display them with pride to strangers saying that for this head one of their ancestors, or his father, or the man himself refused the offer of a large sum of money."

HEAD COLLECTING

This gruesome practice was rooted in the deep Celtic belief that the human soul resided in the head. When a Celtic warrior kept the head of his enemy, he was honoring the man's bravery and spirit. Probably he believed that he was also keeping some of that spirit for himself, and that it would help protect his home and family. And of course, hanging up the heads of dead enemies outside the house was a good way for a warrior to advertise his strength and skill in battle. But more importantly, the head, as the container of the soul, was extremely powerful—perhaps almost divine. For this reason human heads were among the most common designs in Celtic artwork. They remained so for a long time, even decorating the doorways of some medieval Irish churches.

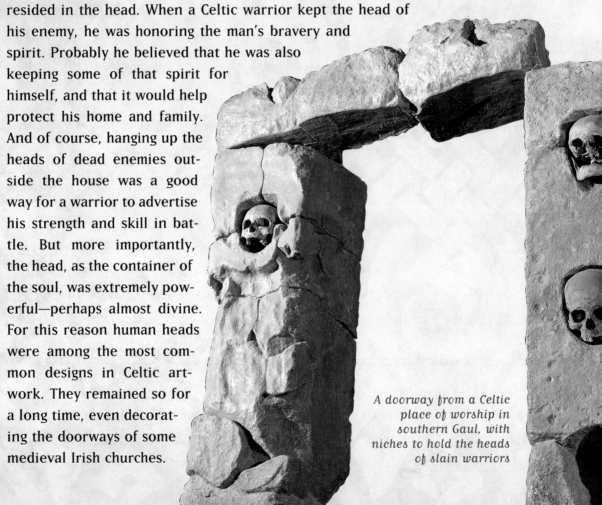

A doorway from a Celtic place of worship in southern Gaul, with niches to hold the heads of slain warriors

CAESAR

In the 60s BCE a Germanic tribe, the Suebi, was making serious inroads into Gaul, and eastern Celtic tribes were being pushed westward by the Dacians. The Helvetii, who lived in what is now Switzerland, came under so much pressure from both north and east that the whole tribe decided to migrate to western Gaul and resettle near the Atlantic Ocean. They prepared carefully, even taking a census "name by name . . . of those who were able to bear arms; and likewise the boys, the old men, and the women, separately." As reported by Julius Caesar, who later found this document, it was written in Greek letters and gave the total number of emigrants as 368,000.

In 59 BCE Caesar became governor of Roman Gaul. So when the Helvetii wanted to pass through this area on their way west, they had to ask his permission. He refused. They went through Aedui terri-tory instead—and the Aedui turned to Caesar to help them deal with this invasion. As governor, Caesar had legions under his command,

Gaulish warriors in the midst of battle, from a nineteenth-century book illustration

and he was only too happy to lead them against the Helvetii. In 58 BCE he followed the Helvetii into "Long-Haired Gaul," defeated them near Bibracte, and sent the 110,000 survivors back where they had come from.

At this point Caesar, too, should have gone back where he came from. Instead, he and his army advanced deeper into Gaul. He claimed that as Protector of Gaul, he had a duty to drive out the Germans who had established themselves there. He did so. And then he settled down for the winter in Bibracte, and began writing his *Commentaries on the Gallic War*, dispatches that he sent back to Rome like press releases.

In debt and ambitious, Caesar had found a golden opportunity—literally—to improve his fortunes. Gaul was rich in land and resources and markets (Roman merchants did a booming business in Celtic cities). Moreover, the Celts had hundreds of gold mines, some of them very large-scale operations indeed. If Caesar could conquer Gaul, he would not only gain a reputation as a great general but would also be able to seize much of its wealth. This was a surefire route to power in Rome.

A northern tribe, the Belgae, were first to react to Caesar's move into Gaul and rise against him. He defeated them in a fierce battle in 57 BCE, then headed west to subdue the other outlying tribes. This way he had central Gaul encircled, cutting it off from outside supplies and assistance. The Celtic tribes were unable to overcome their differences and unite against Caesar, and by the end of 56 BCE all of Gaul was his. He was starting to enjoy the prestige and riches he'd sought—in fact, during

Second-century BCE gold coins of the Parisii tribe show a woman's head and a horse.

his years in Gaul he acquired so much gold that its price on the Roman market dropped by one-sixth.

In 55 and 54 BCE Caesar made two brief forays into Britain, the very edge of the known world, further increasing his heroic reputation back in Rome. But when he returned to Gaul after the second expedition, he found the Celts in open rebellion. They were led by Ambiorix, chief of a tribe in what is now Belgium, whose warriors had destroyed an entire legion. It took Caesar's forces a year of hard fighting to crush the uprising.

Rome did not have access to enough gold to make its own gold coins until Caesar conquered Gaul.

In 52 BCE there was an even more serious revolt. Its leader was Vercingetorix, whom Caesar himself described as a man of boundless energy with iron discipline. Vercingetorix was a noble from the Arverni tribe of central Gaul, and he must have had an unusually magnetic personality because he was able to do what almost no Celtic leader before had managed: unite the tribes. Not only did he have a strong following from among the Arverni, but he gathered together warriors from other tribes as well. As his movement grew, a multi-tribal council voted Vercingetorix war leader in command of all the tribes of Gaul. His army included some 15,000 warriors on horseback who, according to Dio Cassius, all swore that "no member of the cavalry who had not twice ridden through the enemy's army, should ever again be received under a roof or be allowed to see his children, parents or wife."

Caesar reacted to the uprising by besieging and destroying many of the cities of central Gaul. Vercingetorix's forces successfully countered with guerrilla warfare. Caesar, his own cavalry far outnumbered by Vercingetorix's, brought in German horsemen as mercenaries. With their help he and his legions began to close in on the rebels. Vercingetorix and his army took refuge in Alesia, a fortified city atop a high hill

In a dramatic 1899 painting, Vercingetorix throws down his arms and prepares to surrender to Caesar.

between two rivers. Caesar besieged Alesia. A Council of Gauls, as Caesar called it, assembled to gather an army to go to Vercingetorix's aid: 240,000 warriors on foot and 8,000 on horseback, drawn from more than forty tribes.

But while Vercingetorix waited for the relief force, his men were starving inside Alesia, and Caesar was strengthening his legions' defenses. When the new Gaulish army did arrive, it couldn't get past Caesar's troops. From the hilltop the besieged watched the battle rage for five days and saw far more Celts die than Romans.

Then Vercingetorix called a council of his men and said that since he had undertaken the war not for his own benefit "but on account of the general freedom; and since he must yield to fortune, he offered himself to them for either purpose, whether they should wish to atone to the Romans by his death, or surrender him alive." The decision was made: ."Vercingetorix, after putting on his most beautiful armor and decorating his horse, rode out through the gate. He made a circuit around Caesar, who remained seated, and then leaped down from his horse, stripped off his suit of armour, and seating himself at Caesar's feet remained motionless, until he was delivered up to be kept in custody."

With that, the last great hope for Celtic independence in Gaul was crushed. By the time Caesar left Gaul in 50 BCE, he had destroyed more than eight hundred settlements and had killed or enslaved more than 2 million Celts. As for Vercingetorix, he was held captive in Rome for six years, then killed after being paraded through the streets in Caesar's grand triumphal procession.

The EDGE of the WORLD

THERE HAS BEEN MUCH DEBATE ABOUT WHEN AND HOW CELTIC culture came to Britain and Ireland. Was it brought by large-scale invaders or smaller-scale settlers and traders? Did it reach Britain and Ireland independently, or travel first to Britain and then across to Ireland? And how thoroughly did British and Irish society become "celticized"? We are unlikely to ever have definite answers to these questions. But the evidence strongly suggests that the Celts had reached this western edge of Europe by around 600 BCE. There may have been multiple waves of settlement, or perhaps Celtic language and culture arrived in a more or less steady trickle and gradually soaked in.

We have very few ancient writings about Ireland. And, interestingly, ancient writers referred to the people of Britain as Britons, never as Celts, Gauls, or "Gallic peoples." Nevertheless, we know that by the time the Romans met them, they spoke Celtic languages and that their culture was similar in many ways to that of Gaul.

Opposite page: Actor Samuel Butler as the British chief Caratacus in a play produced in London in the 1830s. A fanciful druid temple appears in the background, and bards hold harps and chant poetry on the lower left.

THE BRITONS

When Caesar embarked for Britain the first time, he was going to an almost completely unknown place. Gaulish merchants went there, but even they could (or would) tell him little about the country and people beyond the ports where they traded. Strabo remarked that "Caesar twice passed over to the island, but quickly returned, having effected nothing of consequence, nor proceeded far into the country." Nevertheless, he did get far enough to make some interesting observations, and wrote almost the first historical records we have of ancient Britain:

> The interior portion of Britain is inhabited by those of whom they say that [according to tradition] . . . they were born in the island itself: the maritime [coastal] portion by those who had passed over from the country of the Belgae. . . . The number of the people is countless, and their buildings exceedingly numerous, for the most part very like those of the Gauls: the number of cattle is great. They use either brass or iron rings . . . as their money. . . . They do not regard it lawful to eat the hare, and the [rooster], and the goose. . . .

Britain not only had Gaulish-style houses but also had distinctive round houses with high, conical thatched roofs. Historians used to describe these dwellings as "rude huts," but archaeologists have learned that they were anything but. Constructing them required sophisticated architectural, engineering, and building skills. Most round houses were quite sturdy and long-lasting and no smaller, in terms of floor space, than an average modern house. Many were extremely spacious and some even had a covered porch in front of the door and a gallery or balcony inside.

Caesar took two legions with him to Britain and of course fought against British forces. He noted that the British warriors had "a more

terrible appearance in [a] fight" because they colored their skin blue with a dye made from the woad plant. He also described the way British warriors used chariots in battle:

It took more than two hundred trees and at least fifteen tons of thatch to build this replica of an ancient British "great house."

> Firstly, they drive about in all directions and throw their weapons and generally break the ranks of the enemy . . . and when they have worked themselves in between the troops of horse, leap from their chariots and engage on foot. The charioteers in the mean time withdraw some little distance from the battle, and so place themselves with the chariots that, if their masters are overpowered by the number of the enemy, they may have a ready retreat to their own troops. . . . [A]nd by daily practice and exercise [they] attain to such expertness that they are accustomed . . . to check their horses at full speed, and manage and turn them in an instant and run along the pole, and stand on the yoke, and thence betake themselves with the greatest celerity [speed] to their chariots again.

Caesar added that his men were "dismayed by the novelty of this mode of battle." Nevertheless, wrote Strabo, "he gained two or three victories over the Britons . . . and brought away hostages and slaves and much other booty. At the present time, however,* some of the princes there have, by their embassies and solicitations, obtained the friendship of Augustus Caesar . . . and brought the whole island into intimate union with the Romans"—the "intimate union" being largely that of a thriving import-export trade between Britain and Gaul.

FREEDOM FIGHTERS, QUEENS, AND DRUIDS

By the time of Strabo's writing, most of the Celtic lands of continental Europe and Asia Minor had become part of the Roman Empire. In 43 CE the emperor Claudius decided to bring Britain under the empire's control as well. British resistance to the Roman invasion was fierce but disorganized—the Celts of Britain were no more united than the Celts of Gaul had been before Vercingetorix. In less than a year all of south-eastern Britain fell to the Romans.

Of course, Britain was still full of tribes and leaders who hated Rome. One of these was Caratacus, who came from the mountainous country of western Britain and led countless raids on the Roman frontier. To put an end to this, in 47 CE the Roman army advanced into what are now Wales and Cornwall. They would remain there for several years, battling the Celts.

Some of the British Celts seem to have welcomed the Roman presence in their island. In 51 CE Cartimandua, queen of Brigantia in northern Britain, offered to turn her territory over to Rome. Her husband, Venutius, was defiantly anti-Roman, so Cartimandua deposed him and chose another man to rule at her side. She further proved her friendship to the Romans by luring Caratacus into a trap and then handing him over to his enemies. At this point Cartimandua's people turned

*Strabo was writing some years later, during the reign of Augustus Caesar, 27 BCE–14 CE.

against her, and she fled to Roman protection. Venutius regained his throne. The Romans would have to fight to conquer Brigantia after all.

For the next several years the Roman army carried on campaigns in western Britain. Around 60 CE the Roman governor, Suetonius Paulinus, decided that the heart of British resistance in the west was Môn, or Anglesey. This island just off the coast was a place of refuge and worship and seems to have been a kind of headquarters for the druids, a powerful priesthood. The Roman historian Tacitus tells how Paulinus attacked the island:

Tacitus's account of the Roman attack on the druid sanctuary on Môn is brought to life by twentieth-century English artist Margaret Dovaston.

> Flat-bottomed boats were built to take the infantry across the treacherous shallows. The cavalry used fords, some troopers swimming beside their mounts. The armed enemy crowded the opposite shore. Among them were women, robed in black, hair wild . . . waving flaming firebrands. Nearby the Druid priests, with hands raised, called down terrible curses from heaven. This awful spectacle brought our soldiers up short. They stood as if frozen, until the general broke the spell by shouting how shameful it would be if they were halted by a gang of lunatic women. So the [Romans] surged forward, hemming in the enemy who was burned by his own torches. Paulinus occupied the island, felling the sacred groves. . . .

Benjamin West's 1778 painting The Bard illustrated a popular poem
that told of the tragic death of the last druid in Wales.

IN GAUL, BRITAIN, IRELAND, AND PERHAPS ELSEWHERE IN THE CELTIC WORLD, THE most highly educated people were the druids. Caesar, who was personally acquainted with at least one druid from Gaul, reported that their education took up to twenty years. The teaching was all done orally, and the students were required to memorize a vast amount of poetry and lore.

DRUIDS AND BARDS

Caesar gave a list of some of the subjects they studied: "knowledge of the stars and their motion, of the size of the world and of the earth, of natural philosophy, and of the powers and spheres of action of the immortal gods." As we saw in chapter 3, the druids also taught "that souls do not become extinct, but pass after death from one body to another." Several other ancient writers echoed what Caesar said, and one gave this additional example of a druid teaching or motto: "to honour the gods, to do no evil and to practice bravery."

The druids served a variety of functions in Celtic society. Caesar wrote, "[They] are engaged in things sacred, conduct the public and the private sacrifices, and interpret all matters of religion. . . . [T]hey determine respecting almost all controversies, public and private; and if any crime has been perpetrated, if murder has been committed, if there be any dispute about an inheritance, if any about boundaries, these same persons decide it; they decree rewards and punishments." Other authors noted that in addition to acting as priests and judges, the druids were teachers, philosophers, and healers. They were so highly respected that they could even stop disputes and battles between tribes.

A goddess wearing a torc, surrounded by birds, people, and animals, both living and dead

Druids were at the top of the social order, and most of them were probably born into the warrior class. Closely related to them were seers and bards. The bards were not just poets who made up pleasing rhymes—their poems kept alive the history and knowledge of their people. Bards also used poetry to praise noble warriors and rulers or to denounce those who were cowardly, miserly, or dishonorable. This ability to make or break someone's reputation gave them great power and an important place in Celtic culture.

Boudica, accompanied by her daughters, rides her chariot into battle at the head of her army.

Almost immediately after the fall of Môn, the southeast rose in revolt, led by Boudica, queen of the Iceni. She was, in the words of Dio Cassius, "tall, terrifying, with flashing eyes, menacing voice and a wild mass of yellowish hair falling to her waist; wearing a great, golden neck-torque, a many-coloured dress and thick cloak," and she addressed her troops "spear in hand." Boudica's army—120,000 men according to Dio—had several successes against the Romans and inflicted a huge number of casualties on them. But once again, the discipline of the Roman troops overcame the fury of the Celts. The rebellion was crushed, and Boudica killed herself.

The Romans steadily continued their conquest of Britain. In 84 CE the island's last Celtic army was destroyed. Tacitus imagined the British leader Calgacus rallying his forces before the final battle. This was how Tacitus thought Calgacus might have spoken of the Romans: "Pillagers of the world, they have exhausted the land by their indiscriminate plunder . . . to robbery, butchery, and rapine, they give the lying name of 'government'; they create a desolation and call it peace."

CELTIC SURVIVAL

In all of Britain, only the Highlands and Western Isles of Scotland—regarded as barren lands inhabited by wild tribes—remained free of Roman rule. But across the sea to the west, there was still one independent Celtic land. Ireland preserved ancient Celtic ways right up to the coming of Christianity in the fifth century. Even after that, many Celtic traditions persisted in Ireland for centuries more.

Celtic ways did not die out completely in other parts of Europe, either. There were still druids in Gaul, Britain, and Ireland until Christianity took hold. Medieval Irish judges worked within legal guidelines probably established by the druids. Medieval Welsh and Irish storytellers and scribes passed on poems and tales that preserved pieces (sometimes fairly large ones) of ancient Celtic lore. There were bards in Wales through the 1500s and in Ireland well into the 1600s.

The Celtic languages were also long-lasting. In the fourth century CE Saint Jerome heard them being spoken in both Galatia and Gaul—and he recognized that the two tongues were very similar to each other. In outlying parts of the Celtic world, far from centers of Roman power (or those of later invaders), Celtic languages survived even longer. Cornish was spoken in southeastern England until the 1770s, and efforts have been under way to revive it since the 1970s. Manx, the Celtic language of the Isle of Man (located in the sea between Wales and Ireland), nearly died out in the 1970s, but now it, too, has been revived.

Irish and its close relation, Scottish Gaelic, are still in existence. In Ireland, Irish is taught in all

A bilingual sign in Ireland testifies to the long survival of the Irish language.

schools, and all official documents and signs are printed in both Irish and English. Breton, the Celtic language of northwestern France, is holding on with about a quarter million speakers. More than 600,000 people speak Welsh, the direct descendant of the ancient Britons' language, and the BBC has Welsh-language television and radio stations. There are singers who perform in most of the Celtic languages, and poets who write in them. There are Web sites in all the Celtic languages, including versions of *Wikipedia* in Welsh, Irish, Manx, and Scottish Gaelic.

Some Celtic countries today enjoy greater political independence than they had known for several hundred years or more. Ireland has been an independent nation since 1922. In 1998 Scotland established its own Parliament, which met for the first time the following year. A National Assembly was created in Wales in 1998, but with no power to make laws. Thanks to an act passed in 2006, the Assembly can now legislate on issues affecting Wales, although still only to a limited extent. The Isle of Man, on the other hand, has been almost completely self-governing since the 1700s.

Also in the late 1700s, interest in ancient Celtic history, archaeology, folklore, and religion began to undergo a major revival. This movement has lasted into the present, not only in the original Celtic lands but also in places where many descendants of the ancient Celts have settled,

A farmhouse on the Isle of Man, whose name comes from the ancient Celtic god Manannán

such as the United States, Canada, and Australia. Today it is possible to read stories based on ancient Celtic history; to listen to songs based on ancient Celtic myths; and to buy jewelry, wall hangings, and many other items based on ancient Celtic designs. The Celtic lands and peoples have passed through many changes over the centuries, but the Celtic love of freedom, self-expression, language and music, art and craftsmanship are all alive and thriving and likely to continue on for a long time to come.

KEY DATES IN CELTIC HISTORY

ca. 1300—800 BCE   development of Celtic language

ca. 700 BCE   beginning of Iron Age Hallstatt phase of Celtic culture

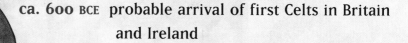

ca. 600 BCE   probable arrival of first Celts in Britain and Ireland

ca. 500 BCE   Celtic immigrants settle in Iberia

ca. 450 BCE   beginning of La Tène phase of Celtic culture

ca. 390 BCE   Celts sack Rome

335 BCE   Celtic ambassadors meet with Alexander the Great

285 BCE   Roman forces exterminate the Senones in northern Italy

281 BCE   Celtic armies attempt to invade Macedonia and Greece

This ceremonial bronze shield was thrown into the Thames River in Britain as an offering.   279 BCE   Celts commanded by Brennus attack Delphi

278 BCE   Three Celtic tribes migrate to Asia Minor

270s BCE   Celtic mercenaries begin serving in Egypt

ca. 233 BCE Galatians defeated by Attalus I of Pergamum

225 BCE Celts in Italy defeated by Roman army at Telamon

218—201 BCE Celtic mercenaries fight for Hannibal
in the Second Punic War

190 BCE Galatians defeated by Rome

133 BCE Rome conquers Celtiberia

124—120 BCE Rome conquers southern Gaul

90s BCE Posidonius's travels in Gaul

67 BCE Galatia becomes part of Roman Empire

58 BCE Caesar begins conquest of "Long-Haired Gaul"

55 & 54 BCE Caesar's expeditions to Britain

52 BCE Vercingetorix leads Gaulish revolt
against Caesar

43 CE Emperor Claudius begins Roman conquest
of Britain

60 CE massacre of the druids on Môn (Anglesey); Boudica's rebellion

84 CE Rome completes the conquest of all but northernmost Britain

*Left:
A massive
gold torc from
Gaul. It may
have adorned
a statue of
a deity.*

*Below:
Human heads
and a triskele
decorate a
silver harness
ornament.*

GLOSSARY

Asia Minor A large peninsula surrounded by the Mediterranean, Aegean, and Black seas. Also called Anatolia, it is the part of modern Turkey that lies in Asia.

Balkan Peninsula A peninsula surrounded by the Adriatic, Mediterranean, Aegean, and Black seas. Today it is occupied by the nations of Greece, Macedonia, Albania, Bosnia, Croatia, Slovenia, Yugoslavia, Bulgaria, part of Romania, and the European portion of Turkey.

Britain The island that is now occupied by the countries of Wales, England, and Scotland.

Carthage A North African city-state that rivaled Rome for control of the Mediterranean. At its height Carthage ruled what is now Morocco, Algeria, Tunisia, and Libya; the Mediterranean islands of Sicily, Sardinia, and Corsica; and southern Spain.

chain mail Armor made of small, interconnected iron rings.

Etruscans People of a group of city-states in northern Italy, whose civilization flourished from about 800 BCE until it was supplanted by the Romans around 300 BCE. Their territory was called Etruria; much of it is now the modern Italian region of Tuscany.

Gaul The Roman name for the area between the Pyrenees Mountains, the Alps, and the Rhine River—modern France, Belgium, and Luxembourg; most of Switzerland; and the westernmost parts of Germany and the Netherlands.

guerrilla warfare Warfare conducted by ambushes, hit-and-run attacks, and similar tactics rather than open confrontation on a battlefield.

Iberian Peninsula The peninsula now occupied by Spain and Portugal.

legion A unit of the Roman army. In Caesar's time each legion probably had about five thousand men.

mercenary A hired warrior, fighting for pay rather than out of loyalty to a nation or cause.

tetrarch One of four rulers who share power equally (at least in theory).

torc or **torque** A thick ring, open at the front, worn around the neck. Celtic torcs were signs of honor and nobility and were usually made of gold. The ends were often ornamented with figures of people, animals, or abstract designs.

FOR MORE INFORMATION

BOOKS

Calvert, Patricia. *The Ancient Celts*. New York: Franklin Watts, 2005.

Grant, Neil. *Everyday Life of the Celts*. Mankato, MN: Smart Apple Media, 2003.

Green, Jen. *Ancient Celts: Archaeology Unlocks the Secrets of the Celts' Past*. Washington, DC: National Geographic Children's Books, 2008.

Hinds, Kathryn. *The Celts of Northern Europe*. New York: Benchmark Books, 1997.

Macdonald, Fiona. *Find Out about the Celts: What Life Was Like for the Warlike Tribes of Ancient Europe*. London: Southwater, 2003.

Richardson, Hazel. *Life of the Ancient Celts*. New York: Crabtree Publishing, 2005.

Wyborny, Sheila. *The Celts*. Farmington Hills, MI: Blackbirch Press, 2005.

WEB SITES

British Prehistory.
 http://www.bbc.co.uk/history/ancient/british_prehistory/
Butser Ancient Farm.
 http://www.gallica.co.uk/butser2/
Celtic Art and Cultures.
 http://www.unc.edu/celtic/index.html
Celts.
 http://www.bbc.co.uk/wales/history/sites/celts/
Simon James's Ancient Celts Page.
 http://www.le.ac.uk/ar/stj/intro.htm
World of the Ancient Britons.
 http://www.gallica.co.uk/celts/contents.htm

SELECTED BIBLIOGRAPHY

Caesar, C. Julius. *Gallic War.* Translated by W. A. McDevitte and W. S. Bohn, 1869. Online at
 http://www.perseus.tufts.edu/hopper/.jsp?collection=Perseus:collection:Greco-Roman
Cunliffe, Barry. *The Ancient Celts.* New York: Oxford University Press, 1997.
——. *The Celtic World.* New York: McGraw-Hill, 1979.
——, ed. *Prehistoric Europe: An Illustrated History.* New York: Oxford University Press, 1994.
Freeman, Philip. *The Philosopher and the Druids: A Journey among the Ancient Celts.* New York: Simon and Schuster, 2006.

Green, Miranda. *Celtic Art: Symbols and Imagery.* New York: Sterling Publishing, 1996.

——, ed. *The Celtic World.* London: Routledge, 1995.

——. *The Gods of the Celts.* Stroud, Gloucestershire: Sutton Publishing, 1997.

——. *The World of the Druids.* New York: Thames and Hudson, 1997.

Jones, Terry, and Alan Ereira. *Terry Jones' Barbarians.* London: BBC Books, 2006.

Livy (Titus Livius). *The History of Rome.* Translated by Rev. Canon Roberts, 1905. Online edition from Electronic Text Center, University of Virginia Library.
http://etext.virginia.edu/toc/modeng/public/Liv1His.html

McCullough, David Willis, ed. *Chronicles of the Barbarians: First-hand Accounts of Pillage and Conquest, From the Ancient World to the Fall of Constantinople.* New York: Times Books, 1998.

Pausanias. *Description of Greece.* Translated by W. H. S. Jones, 1918. Online at http://www.perseus.tufts.edu/hopper/.jsp?collection=Perseus:collection:Greco-Roman

Polybius. *Histories.* Translated by Evelyn S. Shuckburgh, 1889. Online at http://www.perseus.tufts.edu/hopper/text.jsp?collection = Perseus:collection:Greco-Roman

Rankin, David. *Celts and the Classical World.* London: Routledge, 1996.

Ross, Anne. *Druids: Preachers of Immortality.* Stroud, Gloucestershire: Tempus, 1999.

Williams, Derek. *Romans and Barbarians: Four Views from the Empire's Edge.* New York: St. Martin's Press, 1998.

SOURCES FOR QUOTATIONS

Chapter 1
p. 9 "The king received": Cunliffe, *The Ancient Celts*, p. 80.

p. 9 "neither earthquakes" and "in general": Cunliffe, *The Celtic World*, p. 29.

p. 19 "The Gauls, imprisoned": Cunliffe, *The Ancient Celts*, p. 69.

Chapter 2
p. 21 "Gaul under his sway": Cunliffe, *The Ancient Celts*, pp. 68–69.

p. 23 "lived in open villages": Polybius, *Histories* 2.17.

p. 24 "strange men": Jones, *Barbarians*, p. 16.

p. 24 "the haughty answer": Livy, *The History of Rome* 5.36.

p. 25 "with an exclamation": ibid. 5.48.

p. 26 "There were among them": Polybius, *Histories* 2.29.

p. 27 "The whole race": Cunliffe, *The Celtic World*, p. 28.

p. 27 "The Gauls are exceedingly": McCullough, *Chronicles of the Barbarians*, p. 57.

p. 27 "They look like wood-demons": Jones, *Barbarians*, p. 23.

p. 29 "They had learned": Polybius, *Histories* 2.33.

Chapter 3
p. 31 "Massilia was flourishing": Rankin, *Celts and the Classical World*, pp. 39–40.

p. 33 "I will defend": ibid., p. 94.

p. 34 "Portents boding": Pausanias, *Description of Greece* 10.23.

p. 35 "laughed at them": Green, *The Gods of the Celts*, p. 35.

p. 36 "The whole Gallic people": Green, *The World of the Druids*, p. 23.

p. 37 "as the inventor": ibid., p. 23.

p. 37 "It is you who say": Ross, *Druids*, p. 38.

p. 38 "the numbers of Galatians": Freeman, *The Philosopher and the Druids*, p. 46.

p. 38 "to seize" and "There they perished": Pausanias, *Description of Greece* 1.7.

p. 39 "Each tribe was divided": Freeman, *The Philosopher and the Druids*, p.43.

Chapter 4

p. 43 "the clothing of the Gauls": Freeman, *The Philosopher and the Druids*, p. 106.

p. 44 "the people dwell" and "milk and all kinds": McCullough, *Chronicles of the Barbarians*, p. 7.

p. 44 "In the provinces": Jones, *Barbarians*, p. 33.

p. 45 "He divided the land": Freeman, *The Philosopher and the Druids*, p. 132.

p. 45 "invite strangers": Cunliffe, *The Celtic World*, p. 43.

p. 45 "When a large number": ibid., p. 43.

p. 47 "When Gaulish warriors": Freeman, *The Philosopher and the Druids*, p. 109.

p. 48 "The Gauls practice": ibid., p. 112.

p. 48 "They embalm": Cunliffe, *The Celtic World*, p. 83.

p. 49 "name by name": Caesar, *Gallic War* 1.29.

p. 51 "no member": Jones, *Barbarians*, p. 43.

p. 52 "but on account": Caesar, *Gallic War* 7.88.

p. 52 "Vercingetorix, after putting": Plutarch, "The Life of Julius Caesar" 27. Online at http://penelope.uchicago.edu/Thayer/E/Roman/Texts/Plutarch/Lives/Caesar*.html#27

Chapter 5

p. 56 "Caesar twice passed": McCullough, *Chronicles of the Barbarians*, p. 10.

p. 56 "The interior portion": Caesar, *Gallic War* 5.12.

p. 56 "a more terrible": ibid. 5.14.

p. 57 "Firstly, they drive": ibid. 4.33.

p. 58 "dismayed by the novelty": ibid. 4.34.

p. 58 "he gained two": McCullough, *Chronicles of the Barbarians*, pp. 10–11.

p. 59 "Flat-bottomed boats": Williams, *Romans and Barbarians*, p. 145.

p. 61 "knowledge of the stars": Green, *The World of the Druids*, p. 50.

p. 61 "that souls do not": Caesar, *Gallic War* 6.14.

p. 61 "to honour the gods": Green, *The World of the Druids*, p. 48.

p. 61 "[They] are engaged": Caesar, *Gallic War* 6.13.

p. 63 "tall, terrifying" and "spear in hand": Williams, *Romans and Barbarians*, p. 146.

p. 63 "Pillagers of the world": Cunliffe, *The Ancient Celts*, p. 9.

INDEX

Page numbers for illustrations are in boldface

ABOUT THE AUTHOR

KATHRYN HINDS grew up near Rochester, New York. She studied music and writing at Barnard College, and went on to do graduate work in comparative literature and medieval studies at the City University of New York. She has written more than forty books for young people, including *Everyday Life in Medieval Europe* and the books in the series LIFE IN THE MEDIEVAL MUSLIM WORLD, LIFE IN ELIZABETHAN ENGLAND, LIFE IN ANCIENT EGYPT, LIFE IN THE ROMAN EMPIRE, and LIFE IN THE RENAISSANCE. Kathryn lives in the north Georgia mountains with her husband, their son, and an assortment of cats and dogs. When she is not reading or writing, she enjoys dancing, gardening, knitting, playing music, and taking walks in the woods. Visit Kathryn online at www.kathrynhinds.com

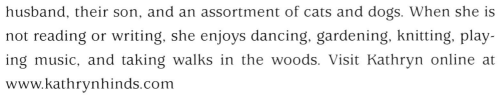

WITHDRAWN